Locker Looks & Study Nooks

a crafting and idea book for
a smart girl's guide: middle school

by Tricia Doherty

★ American Girl®

Published by American Girl Publishing

Questions or comments? Call 1-800-845-0005,
visit **americangirl.com**, or write to Customer Service,
American Girl, 8400 Fairway Place, Middleton, WI 53562-0497.

Printed in China
14 15 16 17 18 19 20 21 LEO 10 9 8 7 6 5 4 3 2 1

Editor: Trula Magruder
Art Direction: Lisa Wilber
Production: Jeannette Bailey, Virginia Gunderson, Judith Lary, Paula Moon, Kendra Schluter
Graphic Artist: Kristi Tabrizi
Photography: Joe Hinrichs
Craft Stylist: Tricia Doherty
Set Stylist: Kim Sphar
Illustrations: Monika Roe and Lisa Wilber

Additional photography: p. 7—© iStockphoto/PK-Photos (dog) and Radlund Photography (girl);
p. 24—Steven Talley (girls) and © iStockphoto/horsemen (horses); p. 28—© iStockphoto/
jannie_nikola (dog poster); p. 34—© iStockphoto.com/elenathewise; p. 38—Steven Talley
(girl) and © iStockphoto/minimil (whale poster); p. 39— © iStockphoto/salihguler (kitten
poster); p. 44—Radlund Photography (girls), © iStockphoto/RuthAnnJohnston (dog), and
Natalia Melnychuk, Shutterstock.com (bunny poster); p. 60—Steven Talley (girls) and
© iStockphoto/minimil (bird poster); p. 61—© iStockphoto/Kudryashka (tree poster),
© iStockphoto/salihguler (puppy poster), and © iStockphoto/lisegagne (fish poster)

Special thanks to Siobhan D., Ciara D., and Fiona W.

Dear Reader,

Design an eye-popping locker at school, create an inspiring study space at home, and prepare top-notch tools for on-the-go events using the colorful projects, quick tips, and innovative ideas inside!

Not only will you learn fun ways to organize your schedule, track your friendships, and manage your classwork, chores, and extracurricular activities—but you'll have a blast doing it!

Quick tips and step-by-step directions will make the projects easy to follow and exciting to explore. Use the ideas as they are, or make them your own. For even more help, look for the cool tools online. Go to *americangirl.com/play* when you see this symbol: play

And be sure to check out your school's policy on decorating lockers before doing anything to yours. If you can't use the locker ideas at school, try them at home!

Your friends at American Girl

CRAFT WITH CARE!

Get Help!
When you see this symbol ✋ in the book, it means that you need an adult to help you with all or a part of the craft. Ask for help before continuing.

When you see the symbol play, go to *americangirl.com/play* for extra printables.

Ask First
If a craft asks you to reuse an item, such as an old magazine, ask an adult for permission before you use it.

Craft Smart
Always work on a crafting table or cover your work surface to protect it. If the instruction says "cut," use scissors. If it says "glue," use craft glue or adhesive dots. And if it says "paint," use a nontoxic acrylic paint. Before using any supplies, ask an adult to look them over—especially paints and glues. Some supplies are not safe for kids.

Put Away Crafts & Supplies
When you're not using the crafts or supplies, store them so little kids and pets can't get them.

contents

locker looks

Think of your locker as your very first apartment. Traditionally, a locker is used to store your books and stash your personal gear, but it can be so much more! Whether you're interested in fashion, sports, science, or anything else, you'll find ideas that will help you turn that plain, empty box into a colorful, charming, and creative "home away from home" that reflects your taste and style.

locker basics

★ If your locker isn't clean when you first open it, disinfect it with a disposable wipe. Then keep it smelling fresh by hanging a sliver of scented soap in a sachet bag or a cute card sprayed with your favorite fragrance! Check with your locker mate about using scented items. She might have a scent sensitivity.

★ If you don't have a locker shelf, buy or make one. It'll keep your books and binders from piling up at the bottom of your locker.

★ Learn your school's rules about what you can attach to your locker. Because most schools don't allow anything adhesive, use magnetic hooks or clips, or attach magnetic sheets to the backs of items.

★ Before you start decorating your locker, choose a theme or style—it will make all your other designing choices easier. If you share a locker, be sure to collaborate with your locker mate.

★ Basic magnetic locker accessories will come in handy. Consider a mirror, a pencil cup, and a dry-erase board.

★ Get to know your neighbors! Since middle schools often combine students from several elementary schools, meeting the people at the locker next door might lead to new friendships.

mini mailbox

Catch cards, notes, and other fun messages in a locker mailbox. To make one, you'll need an empty **soap box.** Snip a small section off both sides and the back. Cut a rounded front if you like. Cover the box with **washi tape.** Write "Mail" with a **puffy-paint pen,** attach **adhesive magnetic strips** to the back, and position the box under the air vents in your locker. Drop in notes from the outside slots to make sure they land in the box. Create boxes for your buddies, too!

hot dots

Jot down your thoughts on colorful dots! Use magnetic dots to write down dates for tests, practices, rehearsals, and other timely topics. To make one, cover a **colorful piece of paper** or **fabric** with **clear contact paper**. Attach the back of the paper to an adhesive magnetic sheet. Then trace a circle on the contact sheet with a **dry-erase marker**, using a **bowl** as a pattern. Cut out the dot, and stick it on the back of your locker or the locker door!

Extra! To keep a dry-erase marker handy, attach it to the dot with a small square of adhesive hook-and-loop fastener. Use a pom-pom as an eraser.

cushy carpet

Cushion your books and other gear on a lush locker rug. Cut a piece of **felt** about ½ inch smaller than the length and width of your locker shelf or floor. Use **craft glue** to attach **2-inch pom-poms** in rows along the felt. After filling up the rug, let it dry for 24 hours. Add **adhesive magnetic strips** to the rug bottom to hold it in place.

Field
Trip
Tuesday

cupcake keepsakes

play Celebrate your friends' special days with cupcakes! Go to *americangirl.com/play* for a **cupcake template**, or draw your own. Then trace the cupcake on a **magnetic sheet**, cut it out, color the holder with **markers**, and **glue** on **mini pom-poms** or **rickrack** for frosting. For a cheer flag, cut out a small **paper** triangle, write a special wish on it, glue it to a **blunt-ended toothpick**, and slip it in the frosting. Hang the cupcake on your pal's locker!

spirit posters

play If a friend has a game or test coming up, show her your support with a **spirit poster**. To make one, go to *americangirl.com/play*, print one of the spirit posters, and personalize it with **gel pens.** (You can also create a poster by gluing cool cutouts to paper and writing your own message.) Stick a square cut from an **adhesive magnetic strip** to each corner, and place the poster on your pal's locker before school starts.

stick around

Give your locker color and texture with appliqués. Cut an **adhesive magnetic sheet** into small squares, and attach one to each **appliqué**. If you like, wrap a collection of the appliqués in tissue paper, and give them to a friend as a back-to-school gift!

wall flowers

Make your locker blossom with
a colorful bouquet! For a vase, cover
an empty **mini candy container** with
stickers. Tape a tiny loop of **string**
to the back of the container, and
hang it on a **magnetic clip.** For each
pom-pom posy, **glue** a **pom-pom**
to a **green straw.** Cut out leaves
from **green washi tape,** and glue
them to the straw. Slip the stems
into the vase.

locker lamps

Design a glam lamp to give your locker light and charm. To make one, cover the globe of a **battery-operated magnetic mini LED tap light** with **washi tape**. Use **adhesive dots** to attach a **beaded bracelet** or **fringed trim** around the light for a lamp shade.

slim trims

Make a show-off shelf with a pop of color and texture. Measure and cut **rickrack, stickers, pom-poms,** or **other trim** to fit across the front edge of your locker shelf. Cut a narrow strip from an **adhesive magnetic sheet**, and press the back of the trim to it. When using stickers, place them along a ribbon or directly on the magnetic strip. Stick the trim along the shelf edge.

17

caterpillar mirror

Smile into this caterpillar mirror—and the inchworm smiles back! To make it, cover a **clipboard** with **washi tape. Glue** a **locker mirror** to the center of the board. Let it dry. For a caterpillar, thread a **large-eyed needle** with **embroidery floss,** and string on enough **pom-poms** to fit across the board. Glue on **googly eyes** and a **felt** smile, and then glue the caterpillar to the top of the board. Cut off extra floss. Add a **pencil case** to the bottom of the board with a hook-and-loop fastener strip. Hang the clipboard on your locker door with a **magnetic hanger.**

Extra! If your locker is really narrow, use a mini clipboard and a smaller mirror and pencil case.

bug bites

play Create a collection of bugs to bite down on important papers until you need them! For each clip, attach a **bug sticker** to **card stock,** cut it out, and stick it to the top of a **strong magnetic clip** with an **adhesive dot.** To use our bugs, go to *americangirl.com/play*.

explore

Recycling
Club
Bake Sale

Bring 2 dozen
cupcakes!

Sparkle

fluffy rug

Bring luxury to your locker with a richly colored rug!
Cut a piece of **grip drawer liner** to the size of your
locker shelf or floor. Using the liner as a pattern, cut
a same-sized piece of **fun fur** or **fleece**. Attach the
liner to the back of the rug with **double-stick tape**.
If needed, stick **adhesive magnetic strips** to the rug
bottom to hold it in place. Add color to the walls with
mini **magnetic decorations**.

Your new glasses ROCK!

Mimi was here

LOL

Be YOUtiful!

message madness

play Trade messages with your locker mate! Use **permanent markers** to design speech bubbles on **dry-erase magnetic sheets.** Cut out the bubbles. (To use our patterns, go to *americangirl.com/play,* and print them on dry-erase magnetic sheets.) Stick the bubbles on your locker. Keep a dry-erase marker and an erasing wipe handy.

Quick tip: If you need only a small amount of fur or fleece, check out the remnant section in a fabric store or large department store.

creative covers

Create a collection of decorative book covers.

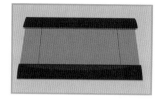

1. Lay a sheet of **paper** on a crafting table—patterned-side down. Place an opened **book** on the paper, mark the book's corners on the paper with a **pencil,** and remove the book.

2. Using a **ruler,** measure and mark 2 inches from the top and bottom marks and 4 inches from the side ones. Connect the outer marks into a rectangle. Cut it out.

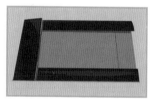

3. Fold the cover 2 inches at both the top and bottom edges and 4 inches at each side.

4. With the book open, slide the front cover into a folded slot. Bend the book toward the spine, and slip the back cover into the other folded slot. Close the book. You may need to adjust the folds.

Extra! Maps, wrapping paper, and shopping bags make great boutique-style covers!

5. Once the cover fits, remove it, and use a ruler's edge to make the folds sharper. Slip the book back inside the cover.

6. Write the book's name or subject on the cover or spine. Decorate the cover with **tape**, **stamps**, or **stickers**.

glitter gallery

Pals, pets, and other pictures will shine in sparkling frames. Cover a **thin adhesive magnetic sheet** with **washi tape**. Place **double-stick tape** on the back of a picture, and center the pic on your sheet. Use a ruler to measure a frame 1 or 2 inches wider than your picture, and cut it out. Decorate the frame with **sparkly tape** or **stickers**.

glamour to go

Transform **plain magnetic organizers** into glamorous beauty tools! Attach **adhesive gems** to a **big clip, storage cup,** or **locker mirror.** Fill the cup with beauty supplies for quick touch-ups.

Great job!

Good for 1 free game day.
From: Ms. Allen

frame of mind

It's easy to frame your thoughts! Just ask an **adult** to remove the cardboard back and glass from a **frame**. Trace the cardboard on a **dry-erase sheet**, and cut it out. Slip the cardboard and sheet back into the frame. Add a **picture hanger** to the back if the frame doesn't have one. Slip a **ribbon** through it, and tie the ends into a bow. Hang the ribbon over a **strong magnetic hook**. Tape one end of a **string** to a **dry-erase marker** and the other end to the back of the frame.

fiesta on board

Add a little *olé* to your day with a flashy board. Layer sheets of **colorful tissue paper** the length of a **brightly colored magnetic message board.** Then cut a long strip of **washi tape** to hold the strips together, and snip the strips into a fringe. Attach one fringed strip to the top of the board and one to the bottom with **double-stick tape.** Use **adhesive hook-and-loop-fastener dots** to add a **pencil cup** to the board, and then slip **dry-erase markers** inside it.

27

gym floor

Take your locker courtside! Measure the length and width of your locker bottom, and cut a **wood-patterned scrapbook sheet** to size. If you like, cover the paper with **clear contact paper,** and add **adhesive magnetic strips** to the back. Slip the flooring on your locker floor or shelf.

Quick tip: If you're an athlete, place a bin in your locker for sports gear. This will keep dirt and sweat away from your other stuff.

Great game!

tied-up pencil cup

Are you a team fan, an athlete, or on a spirit squad? Weave a **really long shoelace** in your team colors through the holes and over the rim of a **magnetic mesh pencil cup,** leaving a tail of equal length on both sides. Tie the shoelace ends together into a knot, and slip the knot over a **strong magnetic hook.** Decorate the front of the cup with a **sporty embellishment.**

Extra! Use a matching shoelace to lash around the edge of a magnetic mesh locker mirror.

makeup monster

Design a glam monster to hold your beauty supplies.

1. Ask an **adult** for a clean **15-ounce can** with sharp edges removed. Make a small **ribbon** loop, and **tape** it to the top outside edge.

2. Measure a 4½-by-9¾-inch rectangle on the back of textured fabric, such as **fun fur,** and cut it out.

3. Apply **double-stick tape** to both ends and the middle of the fabric. Carefully wrap it around the can.

4. **Glue** on **googly eyes** with **fake eyelashes** and a **felt** mouth. Hang the loop over a **heavy magnetic hook,** and fill the can with beauty supplies.

braces case

Keep your braces bright with a locker-sized care kit. Pack an **eyeglass case** or **crafting case** with **dental supplies,** such as disposable toothbrushes, orthodontic wax, orthodontic rubber bands, and soft picks. Attach an **adhesive hook-and-loop-fastener strip** to your case, and stick it to the side of your locker mirror or message board. Decorate the case with **stickers** to match your locker's theme.

home nooks

We all have special places where we do our best thinking. Where's yours? Do you set up a study station at the kitchen table? Settle in at a desk in your room? Or seek out secret spots where no one can bother you? In this section, you'll learn creative ways to track your assignments, organize your supplies, and make your study space more exciting— no matter where it may be!

study-space basics

★ Each week, check your supplies to make sure you have plenty of paper, graph paper, note cards, paper clips, pencils, pens, and erasers. Sharpen your pencils, and fill your stapler. Have a dictionary, thesaurus, and calculator nearby.

★ Have your study space free of clutter. Turn off the phone, TV, or computer—unless you need a computer to complete a project. Say "Study first, surf later," as a way to motivate yourself to get your work done early.

★ Take a half-hour break when you get home from school to eat and re-energize. Then sit at your desk and finish your homework—this will free you up for the rest of your evening.

★ Each Friday, recycle or file papers, empty the garbage, and put away supplies. If you have desk drawers, reorganize or straighten them up on occasion.

bento box

Clear up desk clutter with a **bento box!** Store small desk supplies, such as rubber bands, paper clips, and glue sticks, in the compartments of a Japanese-style lunch box. To decorate the box, use **Mod Podge®** to attach a collage of **paper words and images** to the lid. When you're done, apply a final coat of Mod Podge over the collage. Decorate the sides if you like. Let dry before using.

Extra! If you can't find a bento box, make one! Fill a large, flat plastic container with a variety of smaller plastic boxes.

caddy carryall

Transform a kitchen caddy into a school-supply carryall, and you'll be able to work anywhere—at a desk, a coffee table, or an outdoor study space. Fill a **utensil caddy** with **desk supplies**, such as pens, pencils, a ruler, and a notebook. Decorate the caddy with **scrapbook supplies**, **ribbon**, or **rhinestones**.

chalk art

Start your day with a clean slate—and then fill up the slate! Slap a **large chalkboard cling** on a wall by your desk, and fill it with thoughtful words, dates, and doodles. For an artistic look, use a rainbow of **chalk-marker colors**. Start with something that inspires you, and continue to add more words and drawings.

37

diving board

Fill up a pool-inspired bulletin board with pictures, posters, and more! To make it, cover a 12-by-12-inch cork tile with double-stick tape, and add a same-sized sheet of water-patterned scrapbook paper. For each swim-lane line, string Perler® beads on a stretchy cord, and attach the cord ends to the back of the board with duct tape. Paint wooden clothespins for diving boards, and let them dry. Glue each clothespin to a lane on the board to hold reminders or notes. Attach an adhesive picture hanger to the back of the board, and ask an adult to hang it.

Laugh & pass

What do whales like to chew?

Blubber gum!

dream it, do it.

field days

This bulletin board is a kick to make! Follow the instructions for "diving board," but use green felt or a grassy-patterned paper. Instead of swim lanes, press ball stickers to the tops of pushpins to hang up ribbons, medals, and reminders. Attach an adhesive picture hanger to the back of the board, and ask an adult to hang it.

dots so fun!

Write down important dates, work out math problems, design doodles, or track "To Do" lists with **big and small dry-erase dot clings.** Use them on the wall or your desktop.

tee tote

⭐ Store larger school supplies in a desk tote. To make one, ask an **adult** if you can cut **old T-shirts** into 1½-by-4-inch strips. Slip each strip between 2 holes of a **plastic mesh tote,** and tie a knot. Fill the entire tote or just a few rows. Stock the tote with books, binders, and other supplies, and stand it on your desk for easy access.

Dream
BIG
Dreams

Remember your flash drive, lunch money, snack, or other essential small stuff with a brain box! Drop items off when you get home, and pick them up again on your way out. To make a box, snip the top off a **mini cereal box.** Then measure and cut **decorative paper** to fit around the box. Cover the box with **double-stick tape,** and wrap on the paper. **Punch** a hole near the top edge of each side. Slip a **ribbon** through both holes, and knot the ends inside the box. Decorate with **stickers** if you like. Hang the box on a clip at your desk or on your bedroom doorknob.

great guidelines

Design a wall to hold it all! If it's OK with an adult, use colorful washi tape to create art, write inspirational phrases, frame pictures, or attach a calendar, memo board, or other study tool to the wall. And because it's removable, you can change the colors and designs to suit the seasons!

big book of knowledge

Back up your brain in a binder. Store old quizzes, handouts, tests, and other reusable information so that it's at your fingertips when you need to study. Make tabbed sections by subject. Then perk up the binder—create a cool cover design with wide and narrow strips of washi or duct tape.

web site!

Trap your thoughts on a tangled web!

 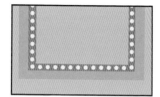

1. 🖐️ Ask an **adult** to remove the glass and cardboard back from a **large picture frame.** Wrap the frame with colorful **washi tape** or **duct tape.**

2. Turn the frame over, and apply **adhesive dots** or **double-stick tape** all around the back edge.

 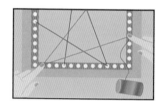

3. Press the end of a **multi-colored ball of cotton string** onto the adhesive. Hold the string down with one finger while you stretch the string across the frame at an angle to the next point—keep the string tight!

4. Then move your finger to that point, and again, stretch the string across the frame to a different point. Repeat the process at random angles until your web is complete. Cut off the loose string.

Extra! Glue spiders to your clips! Purchase small plastic spiders or spider stickers.

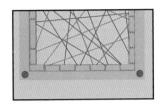

5. Seal the string by using the same tape used to wrap the frame. Apply small pieces of tape around the back edge to cover the attached string.

6. Stick an **adhesive felt pad protector** at each corner. Ask an **adult** to hang the frame. Attach ideas, art, and pictures to the web with **mini clips.**

beauty bin

Turn a plain wastebasket into a work of art! Cut out words or images from old magazines. Use a foam applicator to paint Mod Podge® on your wastebasket in small sections, and then press on the paper pieces. Repeat until you create a design you like. Cover the collage with a final coat of Mod Podge. Let it dry standing up.

paper mate

play Give your wastebasket a friend! Design a paper-recycling bin for your room. Print out a recycling template online, or use ours at *americangirl.com/play*. Cut out 3 of the symbols, and use a foam applicator to paint Mod Podge® on the backs. Gently press the symbols as shown on the outside of a pretty mesh wastebasket. Let it dry standing up.

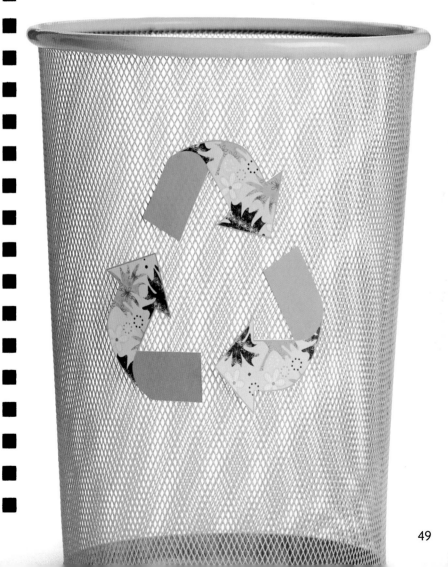

get it together

Don't go crazy trying to pick out clothes each morning. Hang a canvas clothing organizer in your closet! Use file folders to label each shelf. To make the label, open the folder, lay one side flat on the organizer, and then trim the front side to 3 inches. Using a marker, write the days of the week on the folders. Over the weekend, pick out a week's worth of clothes, and place each day's outfit on its own shelf. You can also place important items, such as assignments or books, on the shelves along with your clothes.

picture pocket

Slip a pretty pocket in a picture frame. Ask an adult to remove the cardboard back and glass from an 8-by-10-inch frame. Then wrap the frame in colorful washi or duct tape. Trace the cardboard back onto 3 different colors of felt, and cut them out. Cut one piece 7 inches high and one piece 4 inches high. Layer the felt pieces with the tallest on bottom and the shortest on top. Attach the sides and bottom with fabric glue. Let dry. Reassemble the frame without the glass. Stand the frame on your desk, and fill the pockets!

study buddy

Create a home for a special stuffed friend—and sticky notes!

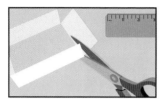

1. To make a home for a study buddy, cut 1 short side off the bottom of a small cardboard jewelry box.

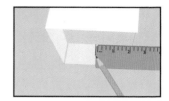

2. Using a ruler, mark the half-way point for each long side inside the box with a pencil.

3. Use the ruler and the tip of a mechanical pencil (without the lead showing) to score that inside line.

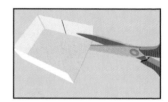

4. Starting at the open end, use scissors to cut down the seam on each side to your marked and scored line.

5. Fold in each cut side to make a roof shape.

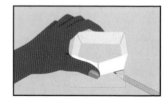

6. While holding the roof together, trace the outside of the roof shape onto the bottom of the box.

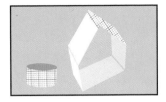

7. Let go of the roof pieces, and cut away the triangles on the left and right sides of the back where you marked them.

8. Pinch the roof together again, and cover it and the outside of the house with washi tape. Cut out a tiny felt rug, and add a small sticky-note pad to the roof.

on the go

You were already busy with lessons, sports, and activities in elementary school. But middle school means even more homework and interests to pursue. To balance all of these demands, you might find times when you'll need to study on the go. The ideas in this section will help you stay organized and ready to study wherever, whenever.

on-the-go basics

★ If you have computer projects that you work on both at home and at school, transport your files with a flash drive. To remember your drive, keep it on your school ID lanyard or in a brain box, shown on pages 42–43.

★ Pack up your backpack each night right after you finish your homework. You'll be less rushed in the morning and less likely to forget something.

★ Walking around with an overloaded backpack can become a pain—literally! To lighten your load, check with your teachers to see if you can access any of your textbooks as e-books online.

★ Clean out your backpack at least once a week to make sure you're not carrying old water bottles, lunches, or damp gym clothes.

★ Add a travel kit to your backpack. You might include lip balm, snacks, hand sanitizer, hair accessories, pads or tampons, or sunscreen.

weekend work space

Take a working surface with you wherever you go. Create a design on a **large portable sketch board** with **washi tape**. To prevent the tape from peeling up, apply a layer of **Mod Podge**® to seal it. Let dry. Attach a **pencil pouch** to the sketch board with a **heavy-duty adhesive hook-and-loop fastener,** and fill it with **school supplies.** Slip the pouch in your backpack when you need to travel.

Extra! If you're working in the wind, wrap a jumbo rubber band around the board to keep your papers from flying.

traveling desktop

On your way to ballet? Waiting for soccer to start? Bored on the bus? Pull out this dinky desk, and get to work! To make it, trim a piece of **heavy card stock** to fit the lid of a **lightweight plastic box.** Cover one side of the card stock with **double-stick tape,** and attach it to the lid. Cover the box sides with **decorative stickers** if you like. Use your portable desk to store **school supplies** or whatever else you might need. Replace the paper once it gets worn.

earbud buddy

Make a cute earbud keeper. Cut **adhesive-backed felt** to cover the lid of a clean **mini candy tin.** Peel the backing off, and attach the felt to the tin. Cut **ribbon** to fit around the edge of the lid, and attach it with **adhesive dots.** Decorate the top with an **appliqué.** Carefully coil your earbud cords inside, and then tuck in the **earbuds**—they won't get tangled!

sweet study center

Design a private study center for your kitchen table or desk!

Display Wall: Start with a **tri-fold display board.** Ask an **adult** to help you cut a few inches off the top so that it's a usable height. Use **double-stick tape** to cover the board with **decorative paper.**

Handy Hanger: Cut **ribbon** strips, and attach them with **adhesive dots** to the back of a painted **craft stick.** Then attach the stick (ribbon-side down) to the board with **craft glue.** Let dry. Use **mini clothespins** to clip notes and photos to the ribbons. For added color, string a few small **beads** along each ribbon.

Poster Pizzazz: Display **mini inspirational posters** on your study board with adhesive dots.

Memo Dots: Use **cork coasters** for mini memo boards. **Glue** 2 together so that they're thick enough for pushpins. Let dry. Paint the coasters with 1–2 coats of **acrylic paint.** Let dry. Attach the coasters with craft glue.

Storage Pockets: Cut the flaps off **used greeting-card envelopes,** and attach them to the board—address-side down —with double-stick tape. Fill with flash cards or papers.

Pencil Bag: Use a **paper gift bag** as a pencil caddy. Attach it to the board with double-stick tape, and fill it with pens and pencils.

middle-school memories

Start storing all your school mementos now, and you'll be glad you did later. First, look for the perfect **paperboard suitcase** or **pretty box**. Gradually fill the memory keeper with trinkets, treasures, ticket stubs, programs, sports ribbons, photos, notes from friends, and other middle-school **mementos.**

What's your favorite study-space tip?

Write to
Locker Looks Editor
American Girl
8400 Fairway Place
Middleton, WI 53562

(All comments and suggestions received by American Girl may be used without compensation or acknowledgment. Sorry—photos can't be returned.)

Mail

Here are some other American Girl books you might like.

Discover online games, quizzes, activities,
and more at **americangirl.com**